THE LITTLE COUCH POTATO BOOK

DIRK DUNDAS

Michael O'Mara Humour

First published in Great Britain in 2001 by
Michael O'Mara Books Limited
9 Lion Yard, Tremadoc Road
London SW4 7NQ

Copyright © Michael O'Mara Books 2001

All rights reserved. No part of this publication may be reproduced, stored in a retrieval system, or transmitted by any means, without the prior permission in writing of the publisher, nor be otherwise circulated in any form of binding or cover other than that in which it is published and without a similar condition including this condition being imposed on the subsequent purchaser.

A CIP catalogue record for this book is available from the British Library

ISBN 1-85479-834-0

1 3 5 7 9 10 8 6 4 2

Compiled by Dominique Enright

www.mombooks.com

Printed in Australia by McPherson's Printing Group

CONTENTS

Introduction	6
What Makes a Couch Potato?	10
The Couch Potato	52
Top Five Things Guaranteed to Freak Out a CP	60
Couches – and Potatoes – in Art	61
A Few Famous Couch Potatoes	66
Quotations for Couch Potatoes	73
Relations of the Couch Potato	76
Crumbs From a Crisps Packet	82
Books for the Couch Potato	91

INTRODUCTION

A Couch Potato is a lazy and inactive person who spends a great deal of leisure time sitting, often eating and drinking, in front of the television. The most popular image is of a lump of a man sprawled inelegantly on a sofa, can(s) of beer to hand, packets of crisps and other snack foods scattered about him on the cushions, perhaps the remains of a pizza or KFC in the grease-spotted box it came in ... And, of course, the remote control perched conveniently near to hand.

This lump is running to fat, his clothes are carelessly thrown on and ill-fitting – generally too small, trousers forced down and shirt buttons straining against a barely restrained, and growing, paunch – he is coarse in feature and in manners. Not an attractive person, a slob in fact.

So, not a lot of people would admit to being Couch Potatoes. Yet many are those – adults and children – who come in from a fairly sedentary day at the office or at school, followed by a journey home for the most part sitting in bus, train, tube or car, to plonk themselves – 'just for twenty minutes' – on the sofa, in front of the telly. Well, poor things, they are tired after a day's hard slog. So mother/wife/partner brings them something to eat and drink while they sit there; or, maybe, they are too tired to prepare a meal so they call for a pizza to be delivered, or they have picked up some ready-made meal on the way home . . . After all, one must get some rest and it's good to relax in front of something not too demanding on those poor brain cells that have been working hard all day. (Have they? Really?)

But of course these are not Couch Potatoes. Are they?

WHAT MAKES A COUCH POTATO?

'Potato' is not a verb, but, facetious objections apart, what makes a Couch Potato is, essentially, a combination of those things that are easily available in the pursuit of leisure and relaxation and that involve the minimum of effort and the maximum of comfort, plus a dislike of activity and a fondness for convenience foods.

The Couch – its relevant definitions:

a) a piece of upholstered furniture

for seating more than one person (however, a Couch Potato has no difficulty in occupying a whole couch – all he, occasionally she, does is sprawl a bit more);

b) a bed, especially one used during an appointment with a doctor or, famously, a psychoanalyst.

The word derives from the French *coucher* which means, as everyone, even a Couch Potato, knows, to put or lay something (in this case usually oneself) down. Sofa so good.

Some synonyms and variants
sofa a long upholstered seat, usually with arms and a back; from the Arabic *suffah* for 'long bench';
settee originally 'settle', when it was usually made of wood with a high back and arms – not really comfortable enough for Couch Potatoes;
divan a backless seat, designed to be set against a wall – not therefore very suitable for CPs; the word – from the Turkish *divan* or Persian *diwan* – can also mean, among other things, a collection of poems or a

Muslim court of law;
daybed self-explanatory – but Couch Potatoes need a back to lean against and arms on which to balance, precariously, such vital items as the remote control, can of lager or packet of crisps;
chaise longue from the French for 'long chair', it is designed for use by one person, has only one armrest and is traditionally reclined on – something which CPs do a lot of, if inelegantly;
chesterfield a sofa, named after a nineteenth-century Earl of

Chesterfield; tightly stuffed and buttoned, so not very convenient as the remote control and other useful objects could slide off on to the floor; then someone would have to be shouted for to pick it up;

récamier a couch, sometimes backless, with a high curved headrest and a low footrest; named after a couch in a painting;

confidante a type of sofa that has a seat at each end separated from the main seat by an upholstered arm;

litter a portable couch or bed, open or closed, mounted on two poles and carried at each end on the shoulders of porters or by animals – this is not seen too often nowadays, but would no doubt meet the approval of the dedicated CP;

palanquin (from the Sanskrit *palyanka*, meaning bed or couch) a covered litter for one (this too would be approved of by Couch Potatoes);

davenport in the United States a large, heavily upholstered sofa (in the UK it is a kind of desk – much less comfortable).

'I am tired of words, and literature is an old couch stuffed with fleas.'
(Derek Walcott, 'North and South', 1981.)

The poet is telling us that the aspiring Couch Potato should avoid literature and make sure his couch is new. Well, perhaps he isn't . . .

'For oft, when on my couch I lie
In vacant or in pensive mood . . .
I watch television.'
(With apologies to William Wordsworth's 'I wandered lonely as a cloud' a.k.a. 'The Daffodils'.)

The Television

'Television is an invention that permits you to be entertained in your living room by people you wouldn't have in your home.' (David Frost)

Defined as an apparatus for receiving and converting radio signals into images on a screen, accompanied by sound, the television set has become essential to nearly every household. Maybe this is why it is known by a multitude of familiar names: **telly**, **TV**, **box**,

gogglebox, idiot box, baby-sitter, tube, boob tube (no, not the garment), **eye, small screen** . . . How most of the names came about is obvious; among the less obvious, perhaps, is '(boob) tube' – this name (don't forget it) derives from the 'television tube' – the cathode-ray tube in the 'box', which is what enables the reproduction of the images you see on the screen. One of the meanings of 'boob' is an ignorant or foolish person, a piece of idiocy . . . the implication is clear.

'Television? No good will come of this device. The word is half Greek and half Latin.'
(Editor of the *Manchester Guardian* C. P. Scott)

The true Couch Potato cannot survive without his (or, much less commonly, her) television, preferably one that includes a VCR so that when not channel-surfing, he (or she) can watch videos – or, indeed, switch from television to video and back again. The phrase 'to have square eyes' is applied to those who are glued to the box for hours on end – in other words, to Couch Potatoes.

Goodman Ace, in a letter to Groucho Marx, wrote of television ('or as we call it back east here, TV – a clever contraction derived from the words Terrible Vaudeville'): 'we call it a medium because nothing's well done . . . and it has already revolutionized social grace by cutting down parlor conversation to two sentences: "What's on television?" and "Goodnight".'

Television's critics and detractors

('zappers' – see below) are numerous, its defenders few, but, strangely, its viewers are countless. 'Chewing gum for the eyes,' the friend of the young son of US journalist John Mason Brown called it (in fact he was referring to some television programmes, not television in general). The American entertainer Ernie Kovacs is supposed to have stated (echoing Goodman Ace): 'A medium, so called because it is neither rare nor well done.' Malcolm Muggeridge called it an 'emanation of human beings' vacuity'. Ever since its arrival people have vilified television. Mindless rubbish, they say, trivializes life, encourages violence . . . They dismiss all the excellent programmes there are, whether drama, documentary, news programmes or films, that have brought so much of the world to so many people – people who would otherwise be that much more ignorant and intolerant.

The average American is exposed to 1,000 television commercials a week, with commercial breaks (as computed by Bill Bryson, *Notes from a Big Country*) occurring every two to seven minutes during programmes!

'Television is more interesting than people. If it were not, we should have people standing in the corners of our rooms.' (Alan Coren)

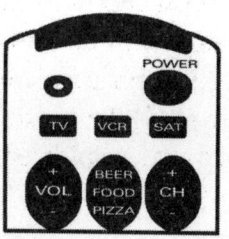

On the other hand, the typical Couch Potato prefers the chewing-gum type of programmes. 'This looks like an intelligent and informative program,' says Jim Davis's cat Garfield. 'Fortunately, there are other things on.'

> Q. How did the Couch Potato get mashed?
>
> **A. He saw a telly across the road.**

The Remote Control

Defined as a device that enables a distant object to be controlled, usually by radio or electrical signals, the most generally used is the one that controls the television – indeed, to many television viewers it is indispensable.

The remote control, many will say, is the villain of the piece. Without it, the Couch Potato would be positively active. Dr Ian Banks, a GP taking part in the BBC's Fighting Fat, Fighting Fit campaign, said: 'Just losing the batteries from the remote control for your television set is equivalent to losing two pounds a year in terms of the extra exercise you do changing channels.' (Losing the remote control itself seems more likely. But whether it's the device itself or its battery that has gone missing, the dyed-in-the-wool Couch Potato will shout for the nearest less inactive person to do the necessary. Shouting can be a form of remote control, sometimes.)

Q. How do you get a Couch Potato to do sit-ups?

A. Tape the remote control between his toes.

The remote control appeals not only because it removes the necessity to get up to turn on the television or change channels, or switch between video and television, but also because it gives its user a feeling of power. Just press a button and the boring politician is obliterated, his place taken by Denise Royle (incidentally, an excellent role model for wannabe Couch Potatoes). Seen that episode? Well, press another button and she disappears, in her place a man behaving badly; erase him and now you can blow up Tom and Jerry. All that, without lifting more than one finger. (A bit like another kind of radio-controlled piece of equipment . . . used to detonate bombs from a safe distance.)

No wonder this gadget is familiarly known as a zapper: to zap is a slang word whose meaning is very much what it sounds like – to attack, kill or destroy suddenly; to deal a rapid, unexpected blow to; to rush, to whiz, or zoom (the kind of movement totally alien to Couch Potatoes); in computing, to erase or clear from the screen; and finally, to fast-forward a video tape or change television channels.

The word 'zapper' is also used to denote a faultfinder or detractor. And the remote control itself is sometimes called 'Frank' – after the rock star Frank Zappa.

One of the reasons God created Eve: He knew that one day Adam would need someone to hand him the remote control.

Q. Why did the couch potato cross the road?

A. To retrieve the remote control that his irate wife had thrown out of the window in sheer frustration at her husband's lazy lifestyle.

The Potato

The potato – the part of the potato plant that we eat – is a tuber, the swollen end of an underground stem.

'The man who has not anything to boast of but his illustrious ancestors is like a potato – the only good belonging to him is underground.' (Thomas Overbury, poet and essayist, 1581-1613)

Originating in South America, where it was cultivated from around AD 200, the potato was introduced into Europe by the Spanish *conquistadores* during the second half of the sixteenth century. Within a century it was a major crop in Ireland, and within another hundred years it was a major crop in continental Europe, particularly Germany, and in the west of England. The Irish economy itself became dependent upon the potato.

In a German prisoner-of-war camp during the Second World War three British prisoners are making their escape along a tunnel. Suddenly they hear the heavy footsteps of an approaching German soldier. One of them spots some large sacks lying in a corner: 'Quick! Hide in those.' Each man wriggles into a sack and when the guard reaches them all he sees are three bulky sacks. He gives one a kick, just to make sure.

'Woof, woof,' barks the Englishman. 'Ach! Just a dog,' the German says. He kicks the next one:

'Meow, meow,' says the Scotsman. 'Ach. A mere cat.' The guard then gives the third sack a kick. 'Potatoes, potatoes,' declares the Irishman.

One of the charms of the potato (the vegetable, that is) is that it can be cooked in an enormous variety of ways. Unsurprisingly, it is a favourite of the CP, especially in the form of chips, crisps and other 'potato snacks'. It is in fact usually a healthy and nutritious food, but Couch Potatoes unfortunately

prefer it in high-fat forms.
For those interested in statistics, a recent survey has revealed that in the UK 'one in three potatoes eaten is a chip', and that the British consume 38,000 tons of chips in a week.

> Q. What's a potato's least favourite film?
>
> **A. M∗A∗S∗H**

The potato is sometimes known as a **tater** (occasionally **tatie**), or, in Scotland, **tatty** or **tattie** (a Central

Scots dialect term, **tattie-peelin**, is sometimes used of people to mean high-falutin, pretentious or affected – perhaps because such people are thought to look upon others as a heap of potato peelings? – not attributes generally applied to Couch Potatoes). It is also called a **murphy**, from the common Irish surname, the potato having been the mainstay of Ireland's economy until the famous and disastrous Great Potato Famine (1845-9).

Q. Why didn't the mother potato want her daughter to marry the famous newscaster?

A. Because he was a commontater.

Yet another name for the potato is **spud,** which comes from a fifteenth-century word, *spudde,* meaning a short knife, which was then extended to apply to a digging tool (presumably used in digging up potatoes).

'We love television,' writes the American columnist Barbara

Ehrenreich, 'because television brings us a world in which television does not exist. In fact, deep in their hearts, this is what the spuds crave most: a rich, new, participatory life.'

Prince Edward Island, Canada's smallest province, sometimes informally called Spud Island, boasts a Potato Museum containing the largest collection of potato-related artefacts in the world. Outside its entrance stands an enormous fibreglass potato.

Q. What do you say to an angry 300-pound baked potato?

A. Anything. Just butter him up.

Q. What did the old Couch Potato say to the new Couch Potato?

A. Son, you're a chip off the old block.

The sweet potato is not related to the potato, and the yam is unrelated to both. A Couch Potato is rarely called sweet unless he (or she) is very young.

Another recent survey in Great Britain has arrived at the disturbing conclusion that one in five under-four-year-olds is overweight, one in ten obese. This is put down to the toddler spending a not always very active day in a crèche or with a childminder, then, at the end of the afternoon being picked up by a busy parent on his or (usually) her way back from work, being taken home in a buggy or by car, then being plonked in front of television/video while said busy parent gets on with chores.

These toddlers might be called sweet potatoes. But not for long.

Q. What do you call a baby potato?
A. A small fry!

A study into the health of children thought to be turning into a generation of Couch Potatoes has warned that schools are failing to give pupils enough time or facilities for sport, and that when the children get home they are unlikely to do anything more strenuous than turn on the TV or play computer games.

The ocarina (Italian for 'little goose', which term might be applied to mini-Couch Potatoes) is a small globular flute which sounds only one or two notes. It is sometimes called a 'sweet potato'.

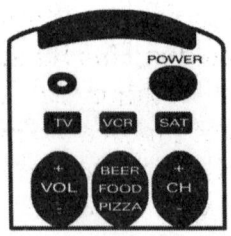

Laziness

'Around the house, I never lift a finger,' sings Homer Simpson, probably the world's favourite cartoon Couch Potato.

Above all, the Couch Potato must distinguish himself (most adult CPs are male) by total laziness and by expecting others – his wife, for instance – to do everything for him once he has done his bit at the workplace. Nothing that so much as smacks of physical or mental effort is acceptable to the committed Couch Potato.

Food and drink should be on hand, and easy to consume. Clothes and footwear should be loose and comfortable so as not to restrict lounging. And of course the remote control must be close by, and working properly.

Curiously, though, research has shown that many Couch Potatoes will expend time and energy by actually getting up and wandering all over the house for hours looking for the remote control, rather than walking to the television and changing channels on the set itself!

Q. How many Couch Potatoes does it take to change a light bulb?

A1. None. They can't be bothered, and they're quite happy watching TV in the dark.

A2. Only one – to shout for someone else to do it.

Food and Drink

Food should preferably be of the kind that can be eaten with the fingers, as forks and knives present rather too much of a challenge. Naturally, the preferred snack foods are those based on the potato, especially crisps. More substantial meals include chips (of course), pizza, burgers, and other convenience foods such as those of the fried-chicken variety. The general preference is for foods with a high fat content. Whatever the reason for this – physiological, psychological or financial – such a diet is the worst for one of sedentary habits, and leads to more statistics:

* Almost 40 per cent of the UK's population never take any exercise.
* Two-thirds of men and half of women in the UK are overweight, while one in twenty Britons is obese.
* Around 54 per cent of Americans are officially overweight while 22 per cent are obese.

James Hill and J. Peters, authors of an article in *Science* magazine, call for governments to take drastic measures to encourage people to exercise more in the battle against obesity, saying that obesity could become a global epidemic and is already at epidemic proportions in the USA.

According to Bill Bryson in *Notes from a Big Country*, the average American walks just 1.4 miles in a week. As one of the surveys already cited has revealed, while 'exercise' seems to have become one of the UK's top leisure pursuits, more people are spending time stuck in front of the television eating snacks. 'Hardly anyone walks. Eighty per cent of journeys are less than five kilometres, yet we choose to take the car,' says the head of the Medical Research Council's Dunn Clinical Nutrition Centre at Cambridge. Which suggests that the British are not far behind the Americans.

Q. Why wouldn't the reporter leave the mashed potatoes alone?

A. He desperately wanted a scoop.

For drinks, just slurp straight from a tin. Cans are handy as they are lightweight and if they fall less spills than would from a glass, and there's no broken glass to sweep up. Besides, beer comes in cans. This is supposedly a favoured drink among Couch Potatoes, even though it has a disadvantage in that the potato does have to get up from his couch from time to time, to answer an inconvenient call of nature.

Q. How does a Couch Potato show that he is planning for the future?

A. He buys two cases of beer.

Q. How many Couch Potatoes does it take to open a can of beer?

A. None. The wife will have opened it before handing it over.

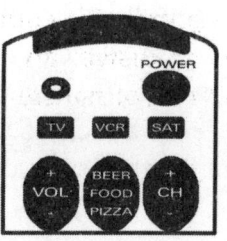

THE COUCH POTATO

Why 'Couch Potato' ... Because:

* The CP lies about on a couch, sofa, divan, or whatever you wish to call it. (For further information, see *The Recline and Sprawl of the Divan Empire* by Edward Maris Piper.)
* The CP is as inactive as a potato.
* The CP, through lack of dietary restraint and exercise, can appear as lumpy as a potato. (Especially, perhaps, because much of his diet is in the form of potato crisps and chips.)

* Like a potato, the CP has eyes (to watch telly).
* Finally, the CP is one who watches the boob tube (remember that?) – a telly addict, a boob tuber. And a common tuber is the potato.

In the early 1980s, the American cartoonist Robert Armstrong drew a cartoon showing a potato sitting on a couch watching TV. Thus did the Couch Potato achieve fame – a club called The Couch Potatoes was formed in the CP's honour, and the television devotee has never looked back.

Q. How do you describe an angry potato?

A. Boiling mad.

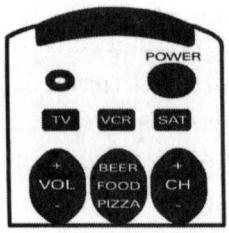

Top Ten birthday presents for a Couch Potato

Annual subscription to
a TV magazine
Widescreen TV with extra big
remote control
Year's supply of beer and crisps
New cosy sofa with reclinable
feature
'Fetch 'n' carry' robot that brings
food from the kitchen
The services of a servant to open
beer cans, order pizzas, etc.

New supply of Couch-Potato-wear
e.g. baggy tracksuit bottoms, baggy
T-shirt and comfy slippers
Year's supply of daily pizza delivery
Year's supply of batteries for
remote control
Year's subscription to cable/
satellite TV

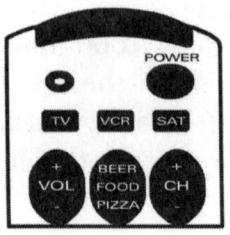

Being a Couch Potato means...

* Having a wide-ranging knowledge of television programmes;
* Being skilled at getting others to bring food and drinks, to answer the doorbell or telephone, to handle any domestic mishap, small or large;
* Having a flexible, agile, and strong thumb. The CP needs this to reach and depress remote-control buttons hundreds of times per day;
* Being able to avoid awkward thoughts and conversations by

concentrating on equally awkward situations acted out on screen;

* Weighing some 20 kilos more than one's more active counterpart, while being able to complain of lacking energy;

* Enjoying at first hand state-of-the-art warnings about health and fitness, perhaps even gaining the opportunity to die early. Indeed, the CP may pride himself on his death-defying lifestyle.

A Couch Potato's favourite sayings

* Never do today what you can put off till tomorrow.
* When in doubt, do nowt.
* If it ain't broke, don't fix it.
* Lookers-on see most of the game.

TOP FIVE THINGS GUARANTEED TO FREAK OUT A CP

- A power cut, and the resulting TV blackout
- Running out of beer and crisps
- Losing the remote control
- Having guests round and being ordered to switch off the TV
- Losing the TV signal when the aerial moves on a blustery day

COUCHES – AND POTATOES – IN ART

You don't need a television to be a Couch Potato. Some of these have been lying on their couches for centuries:

* A fourteenth-century Italian painter, Ambrogio Lorenzetti, depicted two ladies as Peace and Fortitude on a couch, Peace reclining gently, Fortitude sitting demurely upright.

* Napoleon's sister Marie-Pauline appears naked, but lightly covered, reclining sensuously on a couch in

Canova's statue, *Paolina Borghese as Venus Victrix* (1805-7).

* In the sixteenth century came Titian's *Danaë with Nursemaid* in which a voluptuous nude Danaë lies upon her couch, while Jupiter descends to her in the form of a shower of gold (which the nursemaid tries to catch in her apron). Another of his paintings, *Venus of Urbino*, depicts Venus lying on a couch in an enormous room in a palace.

* The eighteenth-century French painter François Boucher painted a

nude sprawling provocatively, buttocks up, on a couch.

* Then there is Jacques-Louis David's portrait of Napoleonic Paris's number-one society hostess, Madame Récamier, reclining coolly on her couch. Her name was later given to a particular style of couch resembling hers.

* In 1865 Édouard Manet's nude Olympia waiting invitingly on a couch was displayed to a disapproving public.

* A few years later another French painter, Edgar Degas, painted his

cousin sitting quietly and decorously on a couch.

* The Victorian soldier, traveller and writer, Colonel Frederick Burnaby, was painted by James Tissot reclining languidly, in uniform, on a couch, smoking and for all the world looking as though he were watching television. (This was in fact probably a rare moment of enforced couch potatoism in a man who was rarely inactive.)

* In 1885 came Vincent Van Gogh's famous painting *The Potato Eaters.*

Q. What does a British potato say when it thinks something is wonderful?

A. It's mashing!

A FEW FAMOUS COUCH POTATOES

* Historically, the most famous Couch Potatoes have got to be the Romans, who seem to have spent much leisure time lying around on couches and eating a great deal. No television . . . but there were spectacles such as chariot races and gladiatorial contests to watch, much more exciting, while slaves ran about pandering to their every whim.

* Matt Groening's character Homer Simpson, who believes that the answers to all of life's problems are to be found on television.

* The Royle, family in Caroline Aherne's acclaimed series about a family who seem to spend all their time bickering around the telly. All aspiring CPs should study Jim Royle who is the classic Couch Potato, sitting in his chair all day, and nagging his wife or son, Antony, to make tea, answer the telephone, and so on. If these would-be CPs prefer, they might emulate his daughter Denise, who is almost as bad, making her husband Dave do everything for her and their baby.

* Jim Davis's cartoon cat, Garfield, known for his trenchant comments, his fondness for watching TV, and for doing as little as possible (Jon: 'Why did we watch that?' Garfield: 'Because we couldn't reach the remote.'); there is even a *Garfield's Guide to Being a Couch Potato*.

* In the cartoon series *Family Guy*, the father, Peter Griffin, when at home is typically to be found in front of the TV with his feet up, remote control in one hand, drink in the other, and a snack perched on his tummy. Calls to mind another cartoon telly addict . . .

* A rock band called The Couch Potatoes, with the catchline 'The sweatiest band on earth' (clearly more active than your typical CP).

* In Japan you might find little dolls, seen as talismans, consisting of an almost spherical body with a head; when tipped over these dolls immediately bob back up to an upright position. They represent Daruma-san, who, through years of absolute inaction, lost the use of his arms and legs. Couch Potatoes be warned.

Or should CPs take some sort of encouragement? For Daruma, or Bodai Daruma – who during those years (nine) of inaction was in fact meditating (this calls to mind Garfield: 'Some call it laziness: I call it deep thought.') was none other than the Indian priest Bodhiddharma, founder of zen Buddhism.

* Two footballers indulging in a spot of couch potatoism have discovered some of the hidden dangers of this vocation.

In early 2001, Rio Ferdinand spent

several hours too many in front of the telly with his feet up, with the bizarre result that he strained a tendon at the back of one of his knees. Some three years earlier, Robbie Keane managed to injure a knee as he reached forward for the remote control.

* There are some who have fame thrust upon them for having a certain feature considered to be typical of the CP. Indeed, some Couch Potatoes may well have seen the feature in question starring in a TV and cinema ad for Reeboks. It

depicts a giant belly chasing a man, bouncing on to a motorbike and sidecar, and eventually falling into a river. One of the advertising copywriters responsible explained, 'I got the inspiration when I saw this giant belly coming round the corner. Minutes later my mate Mickey's face followed it.' A 5-foot-by-7-foot copy of the stomach was made out of latex and foam, with enough room inside it for a running man to move it along. No Couch Potato he.

QUOTATIONS FOR COUCH POTATOES

'It is better to have loafed and lost than never to have loafed at all.'
(American humorist James Thurber)

'There's a good deal in common between the mind's eye and the TV screen, and though the TV set has all too often been the boob tube, it could be, it can be, the box of dreams.'
(American author Ursula LeGuin)

'I do not like work, even when someone else does it.
(American writer Mark Twain)

'Happy is the man with a wife to tell him what to do and a secretary to do it.'
(British businessman Lord Mancroft)

'Laziness is nothing more than the habit of resting before you get tired.'
(Nineteenth-century French author Jules Renard)

'I believe that each individual has a limited number of heartbeats. And I have no intention of wasting a single one on running or exercise.'
(American astronaut Neil Armstrong)

'It is impossible to enjoy idling thoroughly unless one has plenty of work to do.'
(British author Jerome K. Jerome)

'That indolent but agreeable condition of doing nothing.'
(Roman writer and administrator Pliny the Younger)

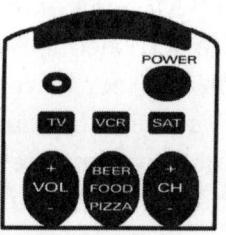

RELATIONS OF THE COUCH POTATO

A sub-species of Couch Potato is the one who instead of watching television, lounges on the sofa playing with a Gameboy. These CPs are usually fairly young, but there is the danger that they will turn into full-blown Couch Potatoes.

Or they might turn into **Mouse Potatoes**. The Mouse Potato is a slightly more active cousin of the Couch Potato. Rather than slump on a couch, he or she will slouch on a chair in front of a computer for hours on end, doing nothing more strenuous than clicking the mouse (the MP's equivalent to the remote control). Mouse Potatoes, especially the most nerdish (in the sense of being a single-minded computer enthusiast), are sometimes called propeller-heads, from jokey depictions of them wearing hats sporting whirling propellers. Among the most obsessive propeller-heads are those known as *otaku*. In Japan this is a derogatory term attached to socially inadequate young propeller-heads who know all there is to know about computer technology but next to nothing about life. The word, meaning 'your home' (because that's where the *otaku* remains day and night) is generally applied to those Mouse Potatoes who spend their time on the Internet surfing through anime clips – high-tech, often violent or erotic, animated films – and the like. In the West, the term is not as pejorative as it is in Japan.

The **Armchair Traveller** (or Armchair General/Strategist/Quarterback/etc.) is a distant cousin, and also an ancestor – there have been armchair experts since well before television, but they gained their theoretical knowledge from books or radio rather than television. Such people always know better than everyone else – like the CP who shouts recriminations at the footballer on the telly.

Q. What does a really evil wife demand in a divorce process (besides the house)?

A. The remote control.

Murder!

Alfred Hitchcock once remarked, 'Television has brought back murder into the home – where it belongs.' Television is certainly where Couch Potatoes come into frequent, probably daily, contact with murder. To them television is where murder belongs. But do they know that, across the centuries, murders have quite often taken place on couches?

* In 1537, Alessandro, Grand Duke of Tuscany, as he slept on a couch, was murdered by his 'friend' and fellow debauchee

Lorenzino de' Medici.
* In 1892 Lizzie Borden allegedly (she was never convicted) bludgeoned her father to death as he was having a nap on a couch. There have been many others, before, between and since. Take care, Couch Potato. Is that a can of lager your dear spouse standing behind you is holding, or is it some other blunt instrument?

Q. Why did the potato cross the road?

A. He saw a fork up ahead.

CRUMBS FROM A CRISPS PACKET

* The word 'potato' is sometimes used to mean a face, possibly because it has eyes, but with the implication that it is less than smooth and beautifully formed ('OK, Dr Jones [Indiana]. Hold on to your potato!').

* A 'hot potato' is a contentious or thorny issue or situation. If you drop something like a hot potato (no CP would accept food that is too hot), it means that you are yielding or giving up on it, usually rather

hurriedly and without question.

* A 'small potato' is a nobody or nonentity.

'What small potatoes we all are, compared with what we might be!' (American writer Charles Dudley Warner)

To 'couch' can mean a way of phrasing or expressing something – we might for instance couch an unpleasant piece of news (e.g. by saying that the telly's broken) in a manner designed not to upset the boob tuber too much (e.g. by saying that the engineer will be round in half an hour, and here's Dave come to discuss last night's match).

'Couch' (in this case often pronounced 'cooch') is also a kind of grass; this, however, is of little interest to Couch Potatoes, who prefer to sit on comfortable upholstered pieces of furniture than on grass. Indeed, many of them rather dislike grass as, if they have a garden, they are probably expected to mow the lawn. Such people are eagerly awaiting the day they can do so with a radio-control device.

* A psychoanalyst is sometimes called a 'couch doctor'.

* A casting couch is indeed a couch – one in a film director's office on which, tradition has it, aspiring actresses are seduced by the director (after which he may reward them with a small part in a film).

* A couch can be a layer or coating – as in a couch of paint. (The Couch Potato avoids any mention of paint,

in case 'the wife' remembers it's time for a spot of redecoration.)

* *Famous couches who were not potatoes:* The British poet and anthologist **Sir Arthur Thomas Quiller-Couch** ('**Q**'; 1863-1944), and the British mathematician and astronomer, **John Couch Adams** (1819-92)

* *A famous potato who was not a couch:* Captain D. J. Jones became known as **Potato Jones** after he tried, in 1937, to run General Franco's blockade off Spain with a steamer loaded with potatoes.

* An article in the *US News & World Report* in May 1998 suggested that the drop in the property crime rate might be in part attributable to more people staying home at night to watch television.

* An Indianapolis bus company called **Coach Potato, Inc**. includes among its many coaches, all equipped with numerous utilities, some furnished with VCRs and televisions. The CP can be an armchair traveller, an actual traveller, *and* not miss any of his daily ration of television programmes – all at the same time. Crisps and french fries are no doubt laid on, as pizzas and burgers surely are.

* An American company is marketing a blanket wrap incorporating a built-in pouch for the feet as the **'Couch Potato'**.

* A Wisconsin-based sportswear shop called the **Couch Potato Athletics Store** prides itself on its 'assortment of fine apparel'.

* The singer Skunk Anansie released a CD single called *Charlie Big Potato* in 1999.

* And long before *Toy Story*, Louis Armstrong recorded *Potato Head Blues*.

* The War of Bavarian Succession in 1778–9 was known as the **Potato War** because each side tried to cut off the other's food supplies.

* A film called *The Couch Trip* (1988) starring Dan Ackroyd, Walter

Matthau, Charles Grodin and Donna Dixon should appeal to CPs, being amusing and undemanding, and more entertaining than an earlier film titled *The Couch,* about a psychiatric patient running amok with an ice pick.

BOOKS FOR THE COUCH POTATO

A selected but non-selective list

'Books are very important. I'm sitting on one to get a better view of the TV.' (Garfield)

Canter, Lee, *Couch Potato Kids: Teaching Kids to Turn off the TV & Tune in to Fun*

Davis, Jim, *Garfield's Guide to Being a Couch Potato*

Lance, Steven. *Written Out of Television: The Complete Couch Potato's Guide to CastChanges & Character Replacements, 1945-1994*

MacNelly, Jeff, *From Couch Potato to Mouse Potato: Successful Tips for the Technically Impaired*

Mingo, Jack, *The Official Couch Potato Handbook*

Murphy, Jane and Karen Tucker, *Stay Tuned!: Raising Media-Savvy Kids in the Age of the Channel-Surfing Couch Potato*

Pitter, Ruth, *The Rude Potato*
Sandburg, Carl, *Potato Face*
Wagner, Cheryl, *The Big Comfy Couch Potato: A Book about Get-up-&-Go*

Michael O'Mara Humour

Now you can order other little books directly from Michael O'Mara Books.

All at £1.99 each including postage (UK only)

The Little Book of Farting – ISBN 1-85479-445-0
The Little Book of Stupid Men – ISBN 1-85479-454-X
The Little Toilet Book – ISBN 1-85479- 456-6
The Little Book of Venom – ISBN 1-85479-446-9
The Little Book of Pants – ISBN 1-85479-477-9
The Little Book of Pants 2 – ISBN 1-85479-557-0
The Little Book of Bums – ISBN 1-85479-561-9
The Little Book of Revenge – ISBN 1-85479-562-7
The Little Book of Voodoo – ISBN 1-85479-560-0
The Little Book of Blondes – ISBN 1-85479-558-9
The Little Book of Magical Love Spells – ISBN 1-85479-559-7

WAN2TLK? ltle bk of txt msgs – ISBN 1-85479-678-X
RUUP4IT? ltle bk of txt d8s – ISBN 1-85479-892-8
LUVTLK: ltle bk of luv txt – ISBN 1-85479-890-1
IH8U: ltle bk of txt abuse – ISBN 1-85479-832-4
URGr8! ltle bk of pwr txt – ISBN 1-85479-817-0
ltle bk of pics & tones – ISBN 1-85479-563-5

The Little Book of Cockney Rhyming Slang –
ISBN 1-85479-825-1

The Little Book of Gay Gags – ISBN 1-85479-590-2

The Little Book of Irish Grannies' Remedies –
ISBN 1-85479-828-6

The Little Book of Scottish Grannies' Remedies –
ISBN 1-85479-829-4

The Little Book of Irish Wit and Wisdom – ISBN 1-85479-827-8

The Little Book of Scottish Wit and Wisdom –
ISBN 1-85479-826-X

The Little Book of Popney Rhyming Slang –
ISBN 1-85479-819-7

The Little Book of the SAS – ISBN 1-85479-887-1

101 Really Unpleasant Things About Men –
ISBN 1-85479-881-2
Get Your Coat, You've Pulled! – ISBN 1-85479-891-X
The Little Book of Crap Advice – ISBN 1-85479-883-9
The Little Book of Crap Excuses – ISBN 1-85479-882-0
The Little Book of Totally Stupid Men – ISBN 1-85479-833-2
Welcome to Dumpsville – ISBN 1-85479-880-4
The Little Book of Despair – ISBN 1-85479-818-9

Postage and packing outside the UK:
Europe: add 20% of retail price
Rest of the world: add 30% of retail price

To order any Michael O'Mara Book please call our
credit-card hotline:
020 8324 5652

Michael O'Mara Bookshop
BVCD
32-34 Park Royal Road
London NW10 7LN